Poet, There's a Spark Within You

*A guide to feeling your inner light
and creating embodied nature poetry*

ASHLEY INGUANTA

© 2020 Ashley Inguanta

Ashley Inguanta
Poet, There's a Spark Within You:
A guide to feeling your inner light
and creating embodied nature poetry

All Rights Reserved.

*This book is dedicated to you, Poet
& your wish to help heal the earth
and all the life it supports,
including yours*

Poet, There's a Spark Within You

CONTENTS

Introduction, 9
Creating a Fire, 11
To be Human is to be Part of the Natural World, 17
Feeling Poetry in the Body, 21
Skillful Attitudes to Feed Your Spark, 25
Listening Deeply, 31
Each Piece of the Writing Process Has Purpose, 37
To Finish a Project is to Find Stillness, 41
The Abundance of the Earth and Our Inner Wealth, 47
The Importance of Readership and Support, 51

Epilogue:
My Teacher Says to Start Small, 55

Introduction

I remember being fifteen years old, standing with a curious body underneath the cool, gentle sun. A river rushed in the distance, rising and crashing with a wildness that comforted me. The land held the river, and the land wanted to hold me. I slowly moved my body into the land—its ground, its leaves, its snow, its grass. The air, too, supported me. I slowly moved my body into the arms of a deep care, a deep love, that I call God. I could cup my own light between my palms, and in that light was the light of the earth, of God, of—well—everything.

I was in the Catskills, and until then, basically all I'd even known were Long Island farms (gorgeous in their own way, but not wide open) New York City, and South Florida (not the Everglades, but the built-up beaches). At fifteen, I was a few years in to exploring concepts of sin and redemption, finding a new relationship with God. Instead of feeling shame for my mistakes, I was starting to feel an understanding, and I was also seeing difficult times as opportunities to hold my light anew.

I remember a vast field I could not stop writing about—dandelions, a rolling hill or two, and so much green. I'd never seen anything like it, and I remember thinking, as I looked out the window of my family's rented van, "I didn't know places like this existed anymore." And I felt something new—an opening to be honest in my need for deep love, which I found that day in the earth, and in God, and—even though I may not have seen it this way at the time—in myself.

When I experienced these moments, I knew how important they were. And as I moved with these moments throughout my life, and as I reflect upon them now, I continue to grow.

For over a decade, I've had the honor of teaching creative writing from a holistic, or whole-person, perspective. I use the word "honor" because it often creates ease in my body, providing a pathway to experience a light, a spark—a physical sensation that accompanies peace, or excitement.

    I earned my MFA from the University of Central Florida in 2011, but it was only after I graduated that I learned, to the full extent, how one can thrive in poetry no matter the connection to academia. Around 2011, I was also in the beginnings of my Classical Yoga practice, and with the help of my yoga teachers and professors, I learned how to guide myself through the process of writing a collection of short stories and poetry. Some of my professors encouraged me to teach from the holistic perspective I was gaining, so I did. Many of my students were "with me" — they opened up to the connection between meditation, bodily sensations, and writing. I was lucky to have them by my side, and I will never forget them.

    I did my best to place my student's wellbeing first, and I could see how they tried to do the same for me. I remember how they'd arrange our desks in a circle before I'd arrive to the classroom, how they'd offer me food and tell me to rest, and how—later on in my teaching career—one even inquired about how I, as an adjunct professor, could take home an expensive word-processing program for free from campus.

    I remember how my students experienced comfort in our gatherings—finding courage to be vulnerable in their writing, honoring their struggles and difficulties through the written word, celebrating their strength through the written word, crying, laughing, finding compassion within themselves and among each other.

    After teaching holistic writing in community college classrooms, university classrooms, living rooms, hiking trails, yoga studios, and now over the gift of video chat, I've gathered some of my most vibrant lessons to share. I use the word vibrant because, when I learn these things as a poet, there is a light present in my body, just like the light I felt in the Catskills. I made a promise to myself to only teach what I have learned. With this book, I hope to share with you what I practice.

Creating a Fire

Today I found so many cattails
in the grass, some of the most
strange & beautiful plants
I've ever seen; there was heron,
too, steady as a cloud, & a
blackbird with hidden rainbows
for wings flew past me; it was an honor
to stand alongside the grasshopper,
fire-orange & wonderful, shyly
speaking its right to be here

    Poet, there's a spark within you. I feel my spark when I walk with the grasshoppers, as they pat along each piece of sawgrass in the marsh, as they support each other with their bodies, as they look at me, asserting their life, their step, their place in the wetlands, in Florida, on the earth.
    The spark arises in my body when I listen: to people in my meditation group share their thoughts and feelings, to the bluejays flying outside the home I sleep in, to the lone turtle pawing its way through soft sand, to my breathing, to poetry.
    Sometimes the spark feels like peace to me, but now I'm learning it can also feel like excitement. A softening in my shoulders, a glimmer of life—an energetic release of tension—in my chest.
    With fire comes light. But also, with light comes fire. This guide is intended for those who are open to, or who already feel, an inner light—an inherent goodness—present inside of them.
    This inner light gives us courage to build fires—to create, to give the gift of warmth, of food, of guidance at night. I believe when we experience poetry (as listeners and readers) that moves us, we are

recognizing our inner light, and we feel a spark in our bodies. The same goes for writing: We experience a connection, we recognize our inner goodness, and the spark is there.

Any recognition of this light—like my examples of the grasshoppers and the turtle—can be an invitation to open our awareness, moving into our bodies, and being with whatever sensations are there. Some people call this embodiment, and you are welcome to do so, too. But of course, I hope you will use whatever language makes your heart sing.

Poet: As you team up with this guide, I hope you will think of yourself as a creator the whole way.

At the end of each chapter, you can create by reciting, and embodying, an affirmation.
- You may say the affirmation out loud.
- You may also say the affirmation silently.
- You may also rewrite the affirmation, using language that connects with you on a more personal level.
- Most importantly, before you say each affirmation, connect to a part of yourself that already knows it is true.

Trust yourself, Poet, especially when choosing how much time to place between reading each chapter and practicing its affirmation.

When you say these words, notice what you feel in your body. You can even place your hand to your heart.

Poet, I hope you feel empowered to give intimacy to these affirmations; you can do this by being with any physical sensations that arise, doing your best not to hold on to the physical sensations, but simply being with them, allowing them to strengthen and fade, change and move.

Affirmation: "I am a creator. When I give patience, I am creating patience. When I give love, I am creating love."

Here is some space to write anything you feel called to:

To be Human is to be Part of the Natural World

I stood at the edge of the marsh
& there—a red-winged blackbird
at the tip of a tree; & behind,
a hundred lilies blooming in
black water; & above, a raincloud
so big it could hold everything
we ever were & ever would be

While it's so important to honor and celebrate a human connection to the natural world, I'm slowly learning that to be human is to be part of the natural world, and listening to my body as sacred as listening to a tree, or the movement of a bird.

In a way, I think listening for a spark in our bodies is a lot like honoring our instincts. I like to think of trees honoring their sparks by speaking to one another in their root-language, helping each other defend against predators. I like to think of birds fulfilling their sparks by carefully building nests, by mating for life.

When I give care to my body, mind, and spirit, I am creating care. I believe an animal can feel this care exude from within me when I walk beside them on my hikes, and I believe the trees do, too. And by existing simply (not to be confused with "easily"), the trees and plants and insects and animals share the joy of life with us humans. There are so many ways we inherently have a symbiotic relationship with the natural world.

Poet: Listening to your body is as sacred as listening to a tree, or the movement of a bird. If you feel frustrated or bored by your writing practice today, I invite you to bring to mind this sacredness. From there, I invite you to feel this sacredness in your breath, your body.

Dear Poet, always remember to first connect to a part of yourself that already knows this affirmation is true.

Affirmation: "Listening to my breath, my body, my mind, and my spirit is a sacred practice. It's one of the most important things I can do."

Here are some pages to record memories of experiencing this sacredness. This way, if you get lost, you can come back here and remember how connecting with your sacred light has impacted you.

Feeling Poetry in the Body

I remember canoeing
down a wide river
as the sun set

I was with
a man I loved

We saw wild turkeys fly,
& after nightfall

lightning bugs

We found our way home
by instinct, moonlight
memory

knowing the riverbank
with our hands

    I've written poems about rainbow fish swimming in rivers, pink Florida berries ready to eat, strangers connected by time and a commitment to surviving, droughts, family history that I later realized was not what I was told. None of these poems have seen publication. Some because they are not finished, and others because I did not feel a strong enough spark in my body with them—yet.
    When I'm reading, the poems that stay with me also spark and move in my body. I often wonder if I am doing the right thing by being a poet. The idea of having a substantial readership really scares me, but I also long for readers—to share the spark with others.

I know I am not alone here. Have you ever felt this? To find comfort, sometimes I remind myself that my work is a thing of its own, and I can have privacy while watching it land into readers' hands.

If you feel a pull to share the spark with others, but also have a fear of having a large readership, here's an affirmation you can try. This is important: Remember to first connect to a part of yourself that already knows this affirmation is true.

"As my writing finds its way into the world, I live my private life."

Here is some room for you to give yourself an encouraging talk: how will you feel the fear of having a large readership and write, and publish, anyway?

Skillful Attitudes to Feed Your Spark

I remember walking on a marsh bank
in the pouring rain

A friend walked with me

I was new to the Everglades
then, not knowing the given name
of any bird or grass,

but I understood the language
of that rain, holding my body
underneath storm-clouds,

cooling me, cooling us all,

bringing relief

Nature-loving Poet, I invite you to think of skillful attitudes like this: You wake up in the morning, and loneliness arises. That loneliness is a feeling. It simply arose, like a planted oak seed sprouts. No matter how lonely you feel, there is a part of you that is very strong, that can—in the present moment—take the action of feeding your loneliness-tree with sunlight and rain. From there, you will feel your loneliness-tree transform. Feel for the spark in your body when it does.

I learned this by being a dharma student, by taking a leap of faith and—on those lonely mornings—taking compassionate action toward myself. Compassion is a skillful attitude that can be applied to our life when we are in stress or pain. To take compassionate action, sometimes I relax my body deeply in meditation, and other times I simply validate my feelings by acknowledging them: "This is hard for me," and I do my best not to abandon myself to stories about the past, or fears about the future.

This is not to say that skillful attitudes don't produce feeling; they surely can. But the gold here is this: No matter what you are feeling, there is a skillful attitude you can use to feed your inner light.

An exercise for you: Read a poem silently, to yourself. Do your best to feel the poem as sensations in your body.

If you feel the spark, let it take.

If the spark grows calmly or wildly or somewhere in between, feed it with the skillful attitude of appreciation. You can do this by simply allowing bodily sensations to arise, appreciating the ease, the pleasure, or any other sensations you feel related to the spark, from moment to moment.

If the spark struggles or wanes, or if it disappears, or if it doesn't come at all, I invite you to take the skillful attitude of compassion. You can take compassionate action by saying "This is hard for me," knowing this is temporary, staying with your breath, letting it take you from moment to moment, into something new.

Here, I invite you to explore appreciation and compassion. You are a creator, remember. Write what makes your heart feel warmth, comfort. Maybe look out your window, at a tree, and wait—for the wind, for a bird, for something else. If trees are hard to come by where you are, there's always the earth; but if all that surrounds you is cement, there's always the sky—and all the life that flies in it. In South Florida we have swarms of dragonflies, families of bluejays. Maybe today your comfort will come from the eagle high up above, or maybe it will come to you from the beetles down below, or maybe you'll remember the time a butterfly landed on your body and stayed a while, or you'll recall the edible weeds you ate, growing wildly.

As you connect, I hope you'll remember that you're part of the natural world, too, and appreciating the intricacy of your own being is a way of honoring the blue jay you see, or the dragonfly, or the ant, or the weed, or the worm. Stay with yourself here, Poet, during the joys and the difficulties:

Listening Deeply

My teacher tells me
to place all of my hurt
in a poem

So I write of the wild
orchids

growing from a palm tree

How glorious & unashamed
they are

in their interdependence

    I wrote a chapbook called *The Island, The Mountain, & The Nightblooming Field* quickly, over a period of about two months or so. I have never written a collection that quickly, but at the same time, it didn't feel rushed or forced. I don't know if that will ever happen again, and I am in no way saying that faster is better. What I am getting at is this: I listened deeply to this project, and it found its pace, its voice, and its timing.

    For the most part, I wrote a poem a day. The listening process helped me feel much less alone in the spring, when the spread of COVID-19 reached the level of a pandemic. The book became a companion to move with as the world changed.

    To me, listening deeply means developing a sensitivity to the sensations present in my body, noticing a physical opening, or an ease, when certain emotions arise. I take the opening, or ease, as a sign that I am ready to care for these emotions.

When writing *The Island*, listening deeply meant noticing when I felt inadequate, scared, thankful for my life, enamored with the creativity of blackbirds, the sturdiness of old barns, the wisdom of one untamed horse, the strength it takes to believe in the existence of a nightblooming field. I noticed these emotions, and when I felt a release in my body, I knew the poem was finding itself.

To me, listening deeply also meant realizing that when I used a smaller notebook, the poems found themselves with more ease. I also realized that earlier drafts of a poem are in no way less valid than the published draft: I saved so many drafts, fragments, and I like to think of them as plants waiting to propagate. And maybe some already have, just by coming before the published poem. When I give thanks to that, my writing practice shifts.

I hope your writing practice grows just a bit today, Poet. If you're not sure how that will happen, listen, and wait.

(This is a kind reminder to first connect to a part of yourself that already knows this affirmation is true.)

Affirmation: "I am listening to you, body. I am here."

Here is room to write what you hear, and what you feel, when you listen:

Each Piece of the Writing Process Has Purpose

Sometimes my heart
shatters into a million pieces

& when it does, sometimes
I feel like the bird
outside my window

Doing what it must, lifting
one twig at a time, patiently
building
a nest

Sometimes—in fact, often times—deep listening means waiting. A poet can wait for a word, a line, a stanza, or even a punctuation mark to feel "right" in the body for hours, days, years.

I am currently in the process of writing a full-length multi-genre collection. The process is not quick, like writing *The Island* was. I am not building a fire with palm fur as kindling and new pieces of flint and steel. Writing this collection is like trying to start a fire with a bow-drill post-rain. The sparks are few and hard to come by, and when they start, it's difficult to tend to them. And there is nothing wrong with that. I encourage you to think of moments like these as opportunities to practice the skillful attitude of compassion.

If you feel like your fire is struggling to begin, Poet, you can have compassion for yourself by saying "I'm with you, and yes, this is hard." You can also remind yourself that rushing the process would be even harder. Each piece of the writing process has purpose, no matter its pace.

Affirmation: "My healthy pacing is perfect."

When you connect to a part of yourself that already knows this is true, can you feel a release in your body?

Here, you can give yourself words of encouragement as you wait for your fire to catch:

To Finish a Project is to Find Stillness

Origins of The Big Dipper, as I Remember it:

In a poem, I wrote of my brother finding a watchdog in the night sky

He did not know what he was seeing, but as centuries passed,
I learned what happens to those who hit the ground with four paws
running, never knowing what death is, living in joy

When the world fell apart, I became a beam of light,
a little like my dog
but different; we were not angels, but we were not ashamed

I recalled so many things when I became that light, like how a fern
is one of the only plants that does not flower

and when Alaska was born, I was not the only one singing
and in the sky, I remembered the first snowfall
maybe ever in the world

And contrary to what some may say, we didn't lose anything
when we built our houses, soup on the stove, dogs running about

We always used the big ladle, even now, especially now
so we can reach each other, like we used to—
after a long day, resting on the couch, my head in your lap

Sometimes, I'm learning, the most loving thing I can do as
a writer is to let my work be, especially when the pain I experience
while trying to finish it overtakes me. I am learning how to re-find
my own personal notion of what a "finished work" is; and now, Poet,

if it feels right in your body, I invite you to do the same.

There is something beautiful about allowing a poem, or a book of poems, to *be*—in a way, the work holds a moment of stillness, I've found.

In the past, my writing practice involved allowing in-progress collections to find that moment of stillness. And when I launched *The Island* into the world, I was allowing it to find its stillness, too. If you have an in-progress work (at any stage) that calls for this type of love, I invite you to try your best to give it. Maybe today will be the day your work will find stillness.

Poet, can you feel the part of you that already knows this is true? Try.

Affirmation: "I give love to my writing by allowing it to be."

Here, you have plenty of room to explore how it feels to give love:

The Abundance of the Earth and our Inner Wealth

Later in my life, I met a woman
who played the drums

She taught me about creating
with dirt & seeds

Her cats worked beside us
much like the farm dog
who watched over me
a long time ago

(Thank you for the food
you helped give me.

Thank you for opening me up to
sustenance,
connection,

our inherent worth.)

    As long as we care for the earth, we will always be able to see its inherent value: the natural fire-starters it provides, the food it gives, the materials it contains to make shelter. The earth also gives us color and texture, a true place to create art, poetry. And yes, brilliantly, the earth is a place to form relationships that cross boundaries of age, race, ethnicity, gender, even species (a dog can become a human's best friend, after all). Some even believe the earth is a sentient being, subject to birth and death, disease and wellness.

    Once, a good friend told me to take it on faith: You are worthy. If you choose to see and feel the light of your own inherent worth, open up to the sacredness of your own breathing, allow your sacred breath to connect to the earth's holy existence—your inner wealth will pour outwards, onto the page, beyond the page.

Take it on faith, Poet, you are worthy. Let your inner wealth heal you, and from there, heal the world.

This piece of you that already knows the light inside, that already knows you are worthy, this part of you that takes things on faith and that rests in faith--what does it feel like?

Affirmation: "I am worthy."

Here, you can explore faith and empowerment. If this gets difficult, bring your breath to the forefront of the present moment, letting it guide you:

The Importance of Readership and Support

& I remember sleeping in a hut
painted like the night sky,
waking up to rain, walking
in the swampy forest, warm

We sat around the fire
every night & gave thanks

& made each other coffee
in the mornings

I'll never forget
the way we all
had something
to offer

over & over

a love inside us,
regenerating

    I've learned that some projects need to experience another element of care before they find their close. Sometimes the poet caring for an in-progress project alone, or with a few helpers, is enough. Other times, poets need a lot of help, an entire readership supporting them and their work, for a collection to reach its point of completion.
    We are all familiar with that very critical voice, that voice trying to stop us from finishing a poem, or a book of poems. This voice tells me to be afraid of my own truth. Sometimes, for a project

to find its close, it needs a village to help bring it out of its struggle.

Remember that you are a creator, Poet. Remember that your appreciation, your compassion, your patience, and your love will launch beautiful things into this world.

I hope you will bravely build intimacy within yourself. And as your body guides you within, your body will also help you find your village.

Listen to your body's signs, its encouragements, and its sparks.

I know you can, Poet.

EPILOGUE

My Teacher Says to Start Small

My teacher says to start small,

    so I bring my mind to
    the grasshopper, neon
    orange & climbing
    through the sawgrass,

    & then I understand
    that is beautiful but
    not small enough,
    so I bring my mind to its
    tiny feet, patting each piece
    of sawgrass, and yes,

        that is graceful & light

but not small enough either,
so I think of the grasshopper

breathing, its tiny breath

        that must feel so big to it, sometimes

Thank You

To everyone who helped this book come into being: To the first humans who felt the light and lovingly explored it, to all of the teachers I have ever had, and to their teachers. To the people who made financial contributions and energetic contributions to this project. To Ryan and Monica W. for your kind, encouraging help with editing. To Monica M. for helping me read the Bible when I felt alone that one Easter. To Allison for walking with me in the Florida rain. To Sam, Chris, Genevieve, Amber, Em, Cecile, Mary Beth, Ryan, Bob, John, Laurie, and Elizabeth for believing in me when I felt like giving up, especially this November. To my dharma teacher, Paul, for helping me find the courage to share my love for God with the world.

Versions of these poems appear in Ashley's chapbook *The Island, The Mountain, & The Nightblooming Field*:

    Feeling Poetry in the Body ("I remember canoeing")

    Listening Deeply ("My teacher tells me")

    The Abundance of the Earth and our Inner Wealth
    ("Later in my life, I met a woman")

    The Importance of Readership and Support
    ("& I remember sleeping in a hut")

The poem in Skillful Attitudes to Feed Your Spark ("I remember walking on a marsh bank") is published in *The Writing Disorder*

Ashley Inguanta is a writer and artist. With her writing, she often blends genre, bringing the rhythm, sound, and feeling that anchors her poetry into her prose. In her newest chapbook collection, *The Island, The Mountain, & The Nightblooming Field*, she gives readers poetry that thrives in its simplicity. This is her first guidebook.

www.ingramcontent.com/pod-product-compliance
Lightning Source LLC
LaVergne TN
LVHW042001060526
838200LV00041B/1819